OF ETHER AND EARTH

Nolo Segundo

PREFACE

As in my previous book, 'The Enormity Of Existence', some of my poems focus on universal themes like love, aging, loss, and of course death, the most universal of all. But others, as before, attempt to understand what I was 'shown' a half a century ago when I had what later came to be called a near-death experience while drowning in a Vermont river. Before then, as with many educated young people, I was sure this world was 'all we got' in our brief lives. So when at 24 I suffered a profound clinical depression and the resultant total nevous breakdown, it seemed logical that the only way to end the pain was to end my life. Boy, was I wrong!

Now untold millions throughout history have experienced the paranormal, the supernatural, in various aspects as NDEs. OBEs [out-of-body experiences], premonitions, visitations by dead relatives or friends [who often appear in the flesh, as it were, 3 dimensional; one friend told me when her dead father came to her to comfort her as she fought alone— her partner having abandoned her—stage 4 breast cancer, he first touched her shoulder as he appeared next to her]. All of us may have experienced what I call 'paranormal lite', like that strange thing that happens when you meet someone for the first time and take an instant liking to them— or conversely you dislike or even hate them, for again no discernable reason. I suspect it's even the same with actors on TV or in the movies: why do we take to some while others leave us cold? Because we can somehow sense their personality? Or is it deeper than that: your soul, on some deeply unconscious level, perceiving another's soul. This is what the poets have meant traditionally by the term 'soulmates'.

By now those of you who are militant materialists, scorning belief in an immortal consciousness or a Supreme Being [the 'Magic Man in the Sky' as my good-hearted atheistic nephew put it to me once] will have thrown up your hands and probably walk away, as you walk away from any sense of wonder, just sheer pure lovely wonder as to why our species is so very different, unique really out of millions of species that have evolved over the eons. Science itself creates far more questions than answers, starting with how did that singularity containing all the energy/mass in the Universe start the Big Bang, when time and space did not yet exist? How, as Shakespeare put it, does Something come out of Nothing?

On the other side of the coin we'll call 'Dogmatism', are those who profess belief in God and the soul but only on their terms. Trying to define God, a Being by definition so far beyond us in every conceivable sense, is to this writer as naive as denying even the possiblilty of such a Being. Sadly, humans have murdered other humans just for worshipping in a different way— it would be like killing someone simply because they speak a different language than you do. Some of my poems, like Miasma, focus on this sorry aspect of human nature. But I hope the reader will find most of them to have a 'satori' effect. A friend from England wrote me that she found many of the poems in my first book to be 'lovely and calming'. It is actually the calming effect I hope to achieve, ultimately. And since for most of my adult life I have been aware we are all both immortal as well as mortal beings, ultimately might be the best anyone can hope for. In brief, it is not given to us to ever fully understand the Mystery that permeates the Universe and every life in it while we are in this world. But we should still try to, and so my poems seek always to nibble at the wonder of our human sentience.

Every human being who has ever lived has many people to thank for his or her life, and most never do get thanked. So let me thank a few now: my parents, my teachers [including the lady who taught me how to overcome a severe childhood speech defect], the doctors and nurses who attended to me over the years, my friends, my wife of over 40 years. Finally, my deep gratitude to my publishing house, Cyberwit.net, and my editor, Dr. Karunesh Kumar Agarwal, who by encouraging me, encouraged my soul.

Contents

OF ETHER AND EARTH

Of ether and earth we are made,
not fully one or the other, and
so we always feel untethered,
ever restless, prone at times
to coming apart…
whole nations come apart,
what chance then have you
or I?

Our souls seek the air,
our bodies cling to earth.
We are never one or the
other, we are never at rest.

Some wait for death,
some wait for God….

WHEN THE WARM DAY DIES

When the warm day dies
And the cool night sets in,
Then I'll be there, beside
You my love, feeling the
Heat of a beating heart,
My arms wrapped round
Your empty shoulders as
I whisper silent words of
Love and longing in your
Lonely, unadorned ear....

Vanity And Dust

Vanity and dust,
Dust and vanity—
Is that all we are?
Clashing egos,
Scheming, soulless,
Taking and getting
Only to lose all to
That cheater Death?

When all you love
Will one day turn
To dust, and none
Can beat emptiness,
Then you must pick—
That all is but chance,
Or all is planned, and
Luck is the illusion…
Sentience a cruel joke,
Or a divine-like gift…
And you are a fluke,
Or one tugged by God.

FEAR NOT, DEATH

Fear not death
When it comes for you—
Death is not a monster,
Not even a master, but
A servant, having no more
Choice in the taking of you
Than you have in the going.

And if you are defiant,
Telling lonely death,
"By my hand, not yours,
I will set my fate!",
Death will smirk, laugh,
And say without rancor:
"Take my job, please!
It has never given me
A moment's pleasure.
To be forever feared,
Hated, despised when
All I ever have done
Was to open a door.
But know, proud human
(The only animal who
Disputes my work),
When YOU turn the knob,
Yes, to eternity's door—
It may not lead you
To the same place
As when I open it."

I knew his meaning,
Responding contritely:
"Fear not, Death—
I will resist not
Your silent coming.
I know who issues
Your deadly orders.
Forgive us humans
For our denial- we keep
Forgetting we exist
Always, and this life
Is but a scratch in time."

c.2014

A TOAST TO THE NAÏVE

To all those who think their thinking
Will understand life and love, war
And peace, hate and forgiveness,
Good and evil, hell and heaven…

To the intellectuals who declare
Hope an illusion, belief delusion,
Religion refuge for fools, and
Science as the only true god…

To the socialist and communists
And all progressive people who
Are certain humanity's makeover
Is within reach, perfection awaits
Only the correct ideology, with
Justice, fairness, equality for all
(as long as it's done their way).. .

To the materialists who are bold
And brave, accepting death as
Extinction, life as meaningless,
So proud they know the truth:
What you see is what you get…

A toast to all the naïve, who
see but are blind, hear but
are deaf, feel but are so
insensate of life's spirit
they live like mice in a
magnificent palace…

A SENSE OF GOD

It comes with the light,
Driving darkness to dust,
Breathing life into death,
Freeing all touched softly.

There is a way of seeing
Without eyes, hearing
Beyond human ears,
Smelling a rose before
Its seed is in the earth,
And touching a beating
Heart with unseen hands.

It takes no more than one
Drop of His blood to save
A world lost in madness.

A QUESTION FOR MR. DONNE

If no man is truly an island,
Does that mean we are all linked
By bridges of hope,
Or causeways of despair?

Are we just flecks of dust
In this world—
Or is each soul
A universe in the next?

MEMORIES TRAVEL WITHOUT THE WEIGHT OF TIME

I'm five: lying in bed in the attic room I share
With big brother (though 4 years older, he won't
Climb the creaky stairs at night unless I go first—
His fear of the dark gives me a secret thrill).
Before leaving for sleepland, I like to watch
The shadows flickering across the ceiling, a kind
Of magic made by the reflected headlights
Of the cars passing in the street 3 stories below.

At seventeen I'm making out with my first girl
On the plush sofa in her house while her mom
Sleeps upstairs. We are both virgins, both clothed
And naïve. Suddenly , as I lay her down, I come—
My first orgasm as, strangely, I had never jerked off
(a mystery I still cannot fathom), but oh wondrous
It was to leave my body and step briefly into heaven.

First came the girls, then the women, in droves,
For I was tall and fair and good with words, but most
Of all, I could make them laugh. And I loved them all,
in my way, and I could love none of them—for I was
afraid of the binding, the fastness that love demands.
It hollowed me out, this fear, and I could not see the
Utter blackness it led me to—and pain beyond pain.

At 24 I was reborn that moment I wept for the loves,
And love I had lost. I was not a new man, nor a good man,

But I was a beginning man, my soul taking baby steps
Towards God and the glorious love infused universe.

In my 32nd year I stood in the nave of the little Anglo-
Saxon church, waiting as my bride came down the aisle.
She began crying, I began smiling—my happiest day.
Now 35 years later, it is still my happiest day....

AN ATHEIST'S SECRET LAMENT

O, how I wish I believed!
Shush… tell no one, but
I want so desperately
To believe in You—
And my absent soul.

I would gladly trade
Darwin and Freud,
Marx and that man
Who speaks only
Through a computer,
I would sell all of
Science, and spit on
Proud nihilism for
A second's glimpse
Of Your eternity.

But I cannot believe
That You exist—how,
How can You be real?
To span the vast universe,
To know all, to be in all?
The universe can exist
Without You—it has its
Laws, we have our laws.
We don't need yours!
We're fine—fine,
Just fine….

AN OLD POET'S WALK THROUGH AN OLD GRAVEYARD

He always liked to walk amongst the dead---
for him is was a secret pleasure to imagine
the lives of once breathing, thinking beings.
He would stop at each tombstone, curious
perhaps more than reverent, for he had long
known the body was just a set of clothes
the soul wears in a world where appearences
matter more it seems than what lay inside…

The old man liked to compare his years to
those chalked on each stone, continually
amazed that so many had died with fewer
years on their belts, so to speak—not
that he thought his 73 winters was a lot:
looking back all that time, all the summers
and all snows and all the fallings of dried
out leaves dying dressed in color like kings,
all those memories wouldn't fill a large
basket in that living library called memory.

There was a newish looking gravestone with
one of those wearther resistant photos of a
handsome young man who died in his 24th
year—rhe old man always wondered how
the young die-- by a rare illness, suicide,
or was he doing something he should not
have been doing, and karma took notice?

In the years practicing his little lauded hobby
the old poet found old graveyards to be best,
for old graveyards have markers of lives that
turned to dust a long, long time ago: 100, 200
years for some-- but for the old poet it was as
though they had died yesterday, because they
were new to him, and his mind's eye could
see them living life large in their own slice
of time, in their own worlds, with beauty and
pain, with loss and joy, with grace and fear.

There were so many folks to visit, each one
whose little stone house he stopped by he
introduced himself to, said hello, wished
them well, and wondered about what sort
of life the woman who died at 36 had lead,
or the really old man of 98 with the funny,
old fashioned name—did he regret missing
the century mark, the old poet wondered.

Some graves he did not like to see, for
they were the graves of babies, who
left the world less than a year after
they had entered it with such promise--
some died withing weeks or months,
a few died the day they were born--
all spoke in stone of hearts broken,
of hope stolen, of love taken away….

ALL THE DEAD I KNOW

Let's start with Eric— a nerdy looking kid before
nerds were invented, and only 18 when he crashed
his funny little French car on a lonely back road,
just three days after we graduated high school—
he was so picked on there, a constant target, always
the frozen deer in the headlights of the bullies, and
the near bullies like me who held him in contempt
[it only took me 40 years to ask for his forgiveness].

There's Beth or Elizabeth or Liz- a girl of joy and
grace and a beautiful tan, so full of glee life over-
dosed in her and so she died at 33 from diet pills.
I learned that only when something— Beth?—
called to my mind one morning to read the obits—
one section of the morning paper I never read—
and I saw her name, and I remembered our brief,
deep summer romance, college kids, babies
making love at night by the outdoor pool while
her family roamed around in their huge house,
the sex no doubt enhanced by its environment,
the sneaky, risky thrill of getting caught— but
the strange thing, besides the sudden, unique
urge to read obits that particular day, was that
I grieved for her, a solid heavy grief for a girl
I thought was just a summer fling....

There's Frank, a Vietnam vet, drafted, a teen-ager,
to fight as a grunt in a war on the world's far side
in a land he knew nothing of except that firefights

were sudden and always deadly, and only one side
would prevail— so when the young VC came at him
in the dark with a knife, Frank pulled his own and
stuck it into a young man who mighty have been
much like himself—and fifty-one years later Frank
died when his own heart suddenly stabbed him....

And so many relatives: Barbara—or was it Susan ?—
yes, cousin Susan who died in her 30's of some
little obscure disease, so rare I can't recall its name.
And my other female cousin, Carol, who too died
young—36, I think, of lung cancer, leaving 5 kids—
and in almost every memory I have of her, she's
got a cigarette, chain smoking her way to death's
door, which is where I saw her last, in her bed
at the hospital, her deathbed, as she lay sobbing,
the grief of her own impending death crushing
her frame, or so it seemed, and I could do nothing.

I supose I could have told her that only her body
was dying, her consciousness, her soul would
go on, would leave her racked and wrecked body
and she would wait for those she loved in heaven—
But I didn't, though I knew the soul was real,
knew it since my own near death at 24, yet what
would it have mattered to her then ? — She was
leaving this world, not for extinction but eternity,
yet still she was leaving it behind, with her
kids still in it, the kids she so wanted, and
no words could lessen the anguish, the loss.

So I never told her she would live forever.

AWAKEN ME, O LORD

Awaken me O Lord,
This burden of sleep is heavy—
I know I am dreaming, such a
Long, long dream—but
I cannot rouse my soul:
It sleeps , sleeps, sleeps,
I can but wait and wait and
Wait….

COME AND DRAW STRENGTH FROM ME

Come and draw strength from me
as I build strength from you.
Pay no attention to the flashes of my mind,
paltry upstarts next to a single heartbeat.

There is death across the land,
dead faces on every street corner
but you and I, if we choose to,
can avoid it and create life, full
and rich like creamed milk.

We are not perfected beings, we sing
not the notes of heaven but of earth.
So my heart gropes in the damp night
for yours, listening to its beats
like raindrops on a windowpane
(life's beauty lies in love's sounds).

Ask not why my heart seeks yours—
if I had to guess, it's an act of God.
One thing I suspect, heartily and with reason:
all life and things of life are born in love,
beauty molded in wedlock of constant hearts
and all misery is from love denied – so
come and draw strength from me
as I build strength from you….

CHILDHOOD

When you are in it,
You think it'll never,
Ever come to end—
How could its magic
Simply vanish, gone
With relentless time?
Because time itself is
But illusion to a child,
Something that moves
So slowly you cannot
Understand why the
Grownups keep on
And on about wasting
Time, and how it flies!

Nonsense! you say,
Because you know
Time is a glacier—
Just look how long
Before a birthday
Or Christmas comes,
When days are weeks
And weeks are months.

And in your child-heart
You believe you will
Always remain young
And free of spirit, for
The big people live in

A hard, little world
While you are ruler
Of an entire universe.

DECEMBER'S TALE

It is the turning month,
The time when life sleeps
And our dreams shiver…
When night grows
Bolder, darker, colder,
And daylight seems so
Weak, slight, bending.
But the air that rushes
Into your lungs like a
Horde of ice-dripped
Savages sears souls
Into fully awakening
From summer's trance,
And so we feel more
Alive in December's
Desolation than any
Other time of the year.

GETTING OLD IS STRANGE

It happens when you aren't looking—
Like water wearing down a rock, so time
Cuts your once fine lines, leaving little
Lumps here, a hedgerow of creases there.
You know you move slower, but you think,
It's temporary—someday I'll race my own
Shadow, and maybe even fly to the moon.
But instead your legs feel more like logs
And your heart warns loudly, 'slow, slower'
And your old fears are gone, but new ones
Have come—especially falling—not in love
As when your beautiful form sought another
More beautiful form, and you sweated loss
Before there was any gain—no, now, you
Fear real loss, the body fading, the mind
Entering a strange and terrible new world.
And all your victories, all your triumphs
Are nought but memories, little teases
Of your youth, its grace, its insouciance.

You know you are approaching God, or
His absence, which you fear even more.
Yet the going and the taking is His to make-
You learned that the hard way, the hellish
Way when you were young and invincible.

So now those you love become more gilded
Day by day, and you know as time shortens
They will live on and you are glad and only

Hope they may recall you here or there…
And if the Lord of all the Worlds is kind,
You may be able to keep track, to follow
From afar (or near) those lives you love….

THE PSALM OF WONDER

As a child
you wondered,
you wondered all the time--
you wondered how tall
was the sky, and
how did the clouds
become elephants and
dogs and eagles and
you wonderd how Santa
could move so fast,
being so fat and old,
yet still he got round
the world in just one
night, a sacred night.
You wondered how
grown-ups got so big
and why you were so
little… and when sex
swept suddenly over you,
stealing the last remnants
of your childhood, you
wondered how you would
ever, could ever approach
the one you desired….
Then you wondered what
turns your life would take,
what work, what play,
what friends, what family
you might have, and would

you meet the mark....
As decades climbed one
another, you wondered
how lay the land of old age,
and you wondered ever more
about what dying meant, and
most of all, you wondered
about God—and realized
all your wondering was
really just about Eternity....

IMPULSE

You feel it sometimes,
A slight twitch of the soul,
[Though you don't know
Yet you are part Eternity],
All you can see is the mud
And sweat of earth days—
But if you try, really try, to
Raise your soul, you might
Feel it rise in your time-
Bound body as its seeks
To sing and soar and see
The brightness of Heaven.

A PAEAN TO GOD

Now I understand—
I can never be complete within myself.

Without You my emotions betray me,
my mind counteracts itself—
hope will flee me, despair will eat me…

unless I reach out for Your love
with a child's open arms….

DIAMONDS DEEP IN THE DUST

They are everywhere,
If we would only look,
And bend and scratch
Through the thick dust
Of the weary mundane,
A world too often heavy
With boredom, pettiness,
Even thoughtless cruelty.

But the jewels are there!
Kick bravely into life's dirt,
You'll see them sparkling
Like secret stars in some
Dark, cold, lonely universe:
Red rubies of love, the deep,
Deep blue sapphires of hope
And most precious of all—
Myriad perfect diamonds,
Each an endless soul,
God's eternal treasure….

INTIMATIONS

We are left clues everywhere—
The purring of the Eternal
made by a boundless ocean
as it laps the shore,
the winds as they kiss
your cheeks and lift
the game heart , the sun's
soft touch on open flesh,
its breath warming and pulling
us up, outward to blue sky….

FOR I CAN HEAR LIFE

When our once young selves
turn stale
And old and old and old,
then,
in that beauty
I still see,
I can hear life—
I can hear life
as it calls out
its love song,
its plaintive plea
to my ageless soul….

And when Death makes
its awkward entrance,
my soul—
sudden cut adrift
from its moorings—
will carry that beauty,
that beauty of a life lived,
with all its loves,
with all its joy
and all its tears,
to the next world,
to the next beautiful dream.

THE LOOK IN HER EYES

No, it isn't what you think
when I say I was enraptured
by the look in her eyes—
the eyes were those of a woman
who was dying and knew she
was dying….

I did not know her well—
she was the wife of someone
my wife worked with in the
prosaic world, the world of time
and schedules and appointments,
the world of taxes and getting
and spending and eating and
sleeping and making love (for
the lucky ones), a world filled
with the nightly news and TV
and a relentless social media,
a world that both commands
and ignores—but not the world
this woman was soon to leave
for, on a voyage she must
take alone, and she knew all
this as she lay small and quiet
in her hospice bed—
past speaking any more,
not even to her old husband.

But though quiet as a mouse
or a saint, she yet smiled, at
all in the room it seemed,
though when I went in turn
to say my good-bye to this
near-stranger, I thought,
'She's smiling at me!' and
then I thought, 'She looks
happy!'—but how can that be
I wondered— until her eyes
danced with a light I have
never seen before in human
eyes—it was her soul I knew
that knew, and her soul had
no fear, death being less than
nothing to it: her soul was ready.

A POEM FOR ALL SEASONS

What makes a good poem?
The beauty of its words?
The easy flow of its lines?
How deeply personal? Or
Should it be more universal,
Singing to all of humanity?

Should the poem be easily
Clutched by the mind's hand,
Or is it better to be recondite,
Its meaning hiding, secretive,
Needing a key to unlock what
Treasure there may be found?
(For myself, I like the simple,
Both to read and write, for I
Have lived enough complicated.)

Good poem, bad poem…
What makes one catapult
Exuberantly into your soul
While another is dragged
Down into the basement
Of the unconscious, there
To be forgotten forever.

MISSING NANA

I'm in the decade before the decade
she left the world, and my world.
The world did not mark it,
the world did not miss her
(any more than it will miss me)
but my world of lost childhood does—
my world of sun-gold and ocean-blue,
my own little world reading book after book
whilst sitting like a happy little king
on the porch of my grandparents' old
house on the bay in Ocean City….
I read in gentle sunshine, I read
while breathing pure ocean air
and sometimes smelling a cake baking
in Nana's kitchen and knowing
I was safe, sure, alive….

I'm in the decade before the decade
my Nana left the world, and as I near
the time when—God willing—
I'll be with her again, the 40 odd years since
she left my world compress:
smaller and smaller time itself becomes,
and freer and freer is my once lost soul….

THE LOW HANGING SUN

I went to take out the trash,
the good trash, glass and paper
destined for re-incarnation and
as I stepped outside, the air cool
and pearly white,
the low hanging sun smiles,
throws a late afternoon warmth
over my body, a blanket of silk.

For a moment I stopped to think,
then thanked the low hanging sun
for being there, the last defense
against a cold deep unto death....

In our immense Universe,
walless, ever expanding,
is mostly night,
utter and fearsome darkness,
all pitch-black and cold, a coldness
beyound comprehension or life—-
so the light and heat of every
myriad star is precious, precious....

A MORNING'S WALK

My wife and I walk every morning,
a mile or so—
it's good for us old to walk in the cold,
or in the misty rain, it makes less the pain
that old age is wont to bring to bodies
which once burned bright with youth,
though now I wear braces on ankles,
braces on knees, and I walk slowly
with 2 canes, like a old skier
sans snow, sans mountain.

We passed a tree whose leaves had
left behind summer's green and now
fall slowly, carefully one by one
in their autumnal splendor.

My wife stopped me—
listen she said— but
I heard nothing—shhh,
stand still she said,
and I tried hard to
hear the mystery.

Finally I asked her, knowing my hearing
less than her's (too many rock concerts
in my heedless youth), what we listen for ?

She looked up at my old head, and smiled—
only she could hear the sound each leaf made
as it rippled the air in falling to the ground.

THE SLEEPWALKERS

I know I am asleep,
I want to awaken
But I don't know
How…so I sleep
With eyes open
And brain turning,
Trying to wake,
Myself, you, all
The sleepers as
They dream an
Endless dream
We call life.

We sleep and dream
Dream and sleep, but
We never awaken, not
Even if we win medals
Of gold and silver or
Purple hearts in war—
We sleep and dream,
Dream and sleep all
Between the moment
We are born and the
Time when we die—
Then we awaken….

AN OLD MAN GIVES BIRTH

They come of their own accord—
They cannot be forced,
And will not yield to demands,
Entreaties, not even begging.

Why I ask, after waking up
After a 35 year long nap
Did the poems again begin
Dancing merrily in my old,
Old head? I might as well
Ask why I am alive, or why
God likes to hide his face.

Old man that I am,
I am happy when I
Give birth to them,
Each near perfect
In my eyes, lovely
To behold, a joy
I want to share with
A very busy and very,
Very confused world.

Forgive me, please,
My parental pride.

EVERY HUMAN HEART IS A CHURCH

Every human heart is a church.
A sacred temple, a holy mosque,
And God is found within
In measure to its love.

Some like to say
There are no miracles:
Look around I say
And then see—
A fat baby laughing,
A new cloak of silken snow,
A heart beating 90 years,
A mind seeing inside …..

What is an orchid
If not a miracle?
What is love
If not the wonder
Of the Universe?

LONGING

Wanting, always wanting—
A smile on her lips,
Fall air crisp and cool,
A dancing fire,
On a cold day's night,
A pat on the back,
A whistle in the dark,
A chance to see God
In love's lonely heart.

THE CHAIN OF DREAMS

Suppose you could remember
Every dream you've ever dreamt,
Each with daylight clarity and as
Real as the breaths you take.

Each dream would be like
A little life, feeling neither
Birth nor death, you just are—
You exist in that dream,
In that little life, then again
In another, and so on till
The dreams are myriad,
In thousands and tens
Of thousands, almost
Countless they would
Seem, the lost dreams
You've had, if you could
Have remembered them.

So could not a life be so?
Just a single dream
Amidst a waterfall of
Dreams cascading through
Time, your soul hopping
From one to the next.
Each dream a life,
Each life a dream.

TIME IS A MAGICIAN

Time does magic,
For time is not real,
It is all illusion, a
Sleight-of-hand.

We're tricked by it,
Parceling time into
Minutes and hours,
Days and months,
Years and centuries,
But they don't exist,
No more than a
Border does when
Viewed from space.

You can prove that—
However old you are,
Think back to a very
Early memory, like
Riding a bike or
Tying your shoes
For the first time
Without help from
The grown-ups...
Be it twenty years
Or eighty years ago,
Doesn't it really
Seem like it was
Only yesterday?

LUDIC

English is not a language
One can ever get ahead of—
Just too damn many words!

Like 'ludic' for example:
Playful, in the sense of
Spontaneous, without a
Real purpose. Sooo…
How come I never came
Across it in over sixty,
Yes, sixty years reading
Untold millions of words in
My beloved mother tongue,
The language I love,
The language I married.

Even spell-check never saw it,
Or else why would it underline
Little Ludic in red, like some sort
Of criminal who needs a good
Sorting out, a spell in scary
Word prison perhaps?

But if you try, really try,
You can find sweet Ludic
Laying low, hiding quietly in the
Big fat Oxford Dictionary, lord
And regent of all word books.

He lives there with his cousins:
Ludibrious and that stuffed shirt,
Ludibry, and Ludrico (no doubt
From the Italian side of the
Family) and, of course, the far
More famous Ludicrous who
Seems to want all the spotlight
For himself…words can be
So very selfish too.

LOVE IS NOT KNOWN

Love is not known, and
can never be known.
Love cannot be weighed
Like bullion or flour.
Love cannot be roped—
A wild mustang running
Free, never tethered,
Never corralled—freer
Than the North winds.

Love has its own mind:
It comes when it comes,
Will not hear entreaties,
Will not beg its bread,
For love rules all worlds
And love soaks all life.

Love is a gangster,
Obeying no laws,
Taking what it wants.
And love is a priest,
Making holy life's dirt,
Redeeming then the
Wreckage of hope by
Pouring its holy water,
Quenching all longing

Love is a magician,
 Appearing in two

Hearts at once,
Transforming the
Beast into a man,
Girl into woman—
An alchemist
Changing lead
Into pure gold….

And love can never die.
When the heart it holds
Beats its last beat, then
Love will soar with soul
To the next world, for
Love is the only key
That can pry open
Heaven's heavy door.

ON VIEWING THE CORPSE OF MY MOTHER-IN-LAW

How could this –thing, have been her?
Lying shriveled and small on the bed
As those who loved (and feared) her
Gathered in the bereft hospital room
To let their shock and grief melt and
Mold itself into its own atmosphere.
Her body seemed never to have been
Real, never to have been a woman,
Never to have been young once, and
Surely never to have been a mother…..

And if it had been a body once, housing
A small dragon who could lash out fire
Solely with her harsh and brutal tongue,
Keeping those who loved her at bay and
The rest of us wary, aware of her power,
Her terrible gift for shrinking one's soul,
Then where did she go when her mouth
Froze open as the last breath of a long,
Life left quietly, without fuss or rancor?

Still, though imperfect as you or I, she
Was loved, and mourned and honored.
If God only housed saints, think how
Terribly lonely He would be…..

I DIED AS A CHILD

I died as a child,
Or so I suspect,
And my child-soul
Flew to the very
Sweetest heaven,
Where all children
Play joyfully with
The child of God,
Who loves us as
He did on earth.

When I came to
This life many years
Ago, Jesus was still
My best friend, my
Nightly prayers more
Conversations, like
'How was your day?
Mine was o.k.'

But my prayer
To his Father
Was simple and
Constant: O Lord,
Let me live till my
Next birthday—or
Christmas, if that
Comes sooner.
Then you can take

Me Lord, I just want
To get my presents.

As a child, I never
Knew of a child who
Died, and I never
Told anyone about my
Secret prayer. And
I was not afraid of
Dying—how could I
Be, when all it meant
Was going home to
See my very best
Friend….

WHEN I BRUSH ETERNITY

Rare, rare it is,
yet sometimes
I can feel
God's warm breath
stirring awake my
somnolent soul…
and for a moment
or two
I think I will know
the meaning of All,
but soon it recedes,
that sense of Infinity,
and I'm left hollow,
that taste of Eternity
gone….

MUSIC'S MAGIC

They all speak to me:
Sometimes alone, like
A solo cello with its
Sad, plaintive voice
Tugging at my soul
Like a magnet of
Life's deep mystery.

Or maybe a small
Group will gang up
Into a quartet or
Sextet or even a
Tough octet, eight
Musicians as one
In both fury and
Gentle softness.

But sometimes I
Go all out—I take
On a hundred or
More at once as
They breathe life
Into a vast bold
Symphony by
Mahler, Brahms,
Or scores of souls
Reborn in music,
Music that makes
Magic, coming in

My ears while
Putting a taste
Of Eternity on
My tongue….

CHILDISH FEARS

As a child
I was never afraid
Of the dark.
My big brother was,
And he would wait
For me to lead the way
Each night to the attic
Bedroom we shared.
(If irked by him
That day, I would linger
Downstairs, making him
Wait for his night's repose.)

And in bed I would lie awake
For a time, watching with a
Child's wonder the shadows
Flickering across the ceiling,
Made by the cars passing
In the street 3 stories below.
The way they moved so swiftly,
I thought those dark reflections
Of light might be alive, soldiers
Of the night passing over me.

I had no fear of death either, for
I knew if it came, I would go back
To a very beautiful place, feeling
Heaven I had come from, so to
Heaven I would return (but then

I was still innocent) No , I feared
Only one thing, but it was a huge,
Mighty thing: I feared Eternity.

I saw, in my child's mind, a road
That went on forever, never
Ending, without an horizon
To mark the journey's end.
And I quaked at its infinity.

Now I no longer fear the Endless
For my soul once told me, quickly
And quietly: I am here, without
Beginning, without end, forever.

Then I understood – my soul
Reflected my mortal mind,
My brain that can't recall my
Birth and really cannot fathom
Its own death, for it exists only
And always in the moment,
The indefinable, eternal now.

INTO THE CLOUD OF UNKNOWING

From darkness
we are born
into mist and fog,
deep, deep into
the Cloud of Unknowing
where we can see
only shapes and shades
as we struggle , lost,
fearful, half-blind,
wanting clarity...
seeking God.

I HAVE A MIND!

Mindlessly I was watching
A T.V. show about an android
Who had an artificial soul
When eureka! I realized, for
The first time in 60 years,
That I have a mind!

Silly you say—we all have one.
Yes I respond, but how very
Extraordinary it is to have
A mind: rocks don't, nor stars
Nor honeybees, not even my
Beloved dog, who has a brain,
(and a good one for an animal).
But he lacks a mind. I know
That for certain because he's
Never once asked me ,
"Is there a God?"

SCIENCE AND FAITH

They are not natural enemies,
Nor were ever meant to be.
True, for a time, when faith
Was strong, science was bound,
Cowed, driven down—then,
Science began its growth spurt:
By leaps it enlarged, pulsing,
Tumescent, fed by Galileo and
Newton , Curie and Pasteur,
Sweet old Einstein and young
Oppenheimer with his bomb.

Now Faith is scorned by most
Scientists, an unreasoning as
They see it, closing their minds
As tightly shut as ever did the
Padres of the Inquisition. They
Worship reason, while believers
Drown in imagination, fantasies,
A Big Guy God, a soaring soul?
Show me, they shout, prove it,
They demand—reason be all,
They exclaim! Yet Science grew on
The back of imagination, and Faith
Loves reason like a sister, for we are
The seeing ones, and we are the blind.
We can hear God's whispers, but then
Are often deaf to the pleas of angels.
And what we think we know is never,

Never enough—we are always left
Wanting….so we can repair a torn
And damaged heart, but cannot open
It to love's incessant pulling….

MEANING

A child asks why, why
Is the sun so hot, and
Why is the moon white
And water clear, and
Why do we have to die?

The grown-up asks too,
Why do you not love me,
Why did that happen,
Why do I feel so lost…?

And what does God ask,
 Not so much really—
Just why can't you all
Be kind to one another?
He even sent someone
To tell us this was His
One wish—to love,
To love… and we killed
The poor man for it.

NOW THAT I AM OLD

Now that I am old:
Did I know the gold I held,
the softness of a woman's kiss,
my flesh binding to her flesh,
the look in her eyes as they sought
my hidden soul…?

Now that I am old:
Shall I grieve for my young days
When I swam through the world
Carelessly and oft without grace?

Now that I am old:
Does it matter that I can see
Clearer, feel deeper, love in
Freedom and regardless of
The inevitable sadness life
Blankets us all in— finally?

Now that I am old.

ON BEING HUMAN

It's hard being a human being,
Much easier to be a lion or dog
Or a fish or even a giraffe, and
Much more fun to be an eagle.

It's hard always having to think,
To weigh, to count, to decide,
Perchance to reject, or regret.

It's hard to fit yourself to life,
To make do with what there is,
To slide into a lie, to tell truths.

It's hard to live in your dreams
When dreams slip quietly away,
Night after night, in worlds you
Forget by break of day, though
Some sense may linger, teasing
You that life, this life, isn't real.

It's hard to life with your fear,
Be it petty or grand, catching
A cold to catching your death.

It's hard to see suffering, pain,
Or even mere sadness, any loss
Tears at your unbidden soul....
It's hard being a human being,
Much easier to be a lion or dog.

MEASURING GOD

How are you going to do it?
How do you weigh the Infinite?
How do you measure the Absolute?
How do you test the IQ of Omniscience?

Would you measure God for a suit?
Would you ask His age, or how much
money He has in the Bank of Heaven?
What about race, or His education?
What are His interests, likes or dislikes,
pet peeves, political opinions? ...Or
maybe you want to just ask one thing
only—what are His dreams, his loves?

Only you would ask God such,
only you would try to scale divinity,
only you can breed such arrogance—
the tiger burning bright asks for no
accounting, nor does the deer as it's
slain, not the eagle as it soars nor
the reptile as it slithers—but you
do, you creature of singular gifts.
You want to take the measure of
your Creator, though you've been
told you're made in His image,
something not told to the lion
or the grizzly bear or the butterfly,
and still you want to measure Him—

But why?

Why must you try to always to
put God in a box?

You made untold numbers of idols,
all reflecting your vanity, not His.
And then when he came to you as
one of you, a human being, what did
you do? You could not understand how
God could speak to you so simple and
true, you could not grasp what He gave,
and so, you killed him.

A few of the wisest of you knew, knew
it was never God you wanted to test,
never God you wanted to take hold of,
never God you wanted to understand—
it was you all along you wanted to see,
that thing called a soul which you both
doubted and longed for, that thing even
death could not harm, that Being of air
and light you saw in the man crucified.

IN TIMES OF MADNESS

In a time of madness,
When insanity is scratched
Onto canvas by angry painters
And sold for peanuts while
They breathe but when long
Dead of too much drugs, then
100 million will go flying away
For a picture without beauty
Or humanity or even truth—
For that suicidal artist was
Sainted and now sworn by
All the little experts who
Happily declare his greatness.

In a time of madness, how
Will the sane find meaning
When art is the emperor
Without clothes, naked
And butt ugly but none
Dare speak the truth:
That there is no truth—
Just anger and hate and
Febrile, unfertile ugliness.

In times of madness, people
Follow shells, moving voids,
And have burnt all the maps
And squashed every compass.
They follow only one god, as

It impregnates them with a
Myriad of fears and delusions,
And soon they turn to murder:
A reign of terror, a pogrom,
A civil war, a genocide… or
A simple push of the button.

WHEN TIME RUNS OUT

There will come a time
When time runs out,
And you see your life
In all of its totality, with
Every thought, every act,
All your life's myriad days
Compressed into a point,
A singularity that you'll
Grasp in both sudden
Joy and sorrow, at that
Moment when your body,
So familiar once and
Now some alien thing,
Expires and the soul
You weren't sure of
Now sees some other
World—but which
World ? The one of
Light beyond light,
Love beyond love?
Or will it be that
Darkness deeper
And blacker than
A universe void
Utterly of stars
And planets?

THE CARESS OF WORDS

When I read a poem that breathes,
pulses with its own heartbeat,
relentless, compelling in its own desire—
I feel touched as by another, some
uneen hand brushing my hair,
lips as light as air licking the flesh
near my own sojourning heart…

and I return the caress as my hand
glides ever questing o'er the soft and
solid paper, my eyes rolling over the
printed page like a hawk seeking prey,
looking with the desire of the wild
at the naked words, unclothed by any
convention, unsoiled by any deceit.

A good poem is a lover—
a great poem, a great lover,
the kind you never forget.

O, TO BE A CLOUD!

O, to be a cloud and
wander the sky untethered,
freer than any bird,
as free as the wild winds…
changing shape endlessly,
effortlessly, easing
from a stallion to a lion
to a bear in the minds
of open-eyed children
who love the clouds and
love to watch the clouds
as they dance the sky!

Children and clouds,
clouds and children—
a love affair that ends
as childhood ends
and the once children,
now grown-ups, can
no longer see
the living menagerie
way, way up high
where only
the purest hearts
may go….

THE ETERNAL MOMENT

As a child I thought of eternity as endless,
Days and months and years and centuries
Then millennia and billions and trillions
Of boring, boring years—what would I do
With all the time in the Universe…?

But as an old man I know time is a big liar,
Itself unreal, an illusion born of sweat, fear,
The loneliness of spirit in a material world.

I see now Eternity is always here, next to us,
Within us, the moment none can grasp nor
Measure nor repeat, the endless moment,
That indistinguishable point between past
And future, between what was, what will be,
The soul's singularity, its Alpha and Omega.

And all our fears of extinction
are like wasted breath,
for we are real and time
Is not …
WE are the eternal moments.

MY NEIGHBORS

My neighbors are charming,
An old couple in love through
Sixty some years and six kids.
Phil had been an engineer,
Doubtless with formidable mind
But he was usually reticent,
While Nancy loved conversation.

Her wit I strove to match when
We met by chance at the café
Where the Pie Lady made her
Treats of muffins and pie and
Quiche with cups of rich coffee.
Nancy could turn a pun with a
Flick of her tongue, and always
I was so amazed—they're nearly
Ninety and so engaged with life,
One would think getting old,
Really old, was not so bad—and
Their love has lasted so long,
Undiminished, unblemished….

But now Phil sleeps most of the day
While Nancy wears his coat by mistake
And thinks she is going to the doctor
When her friend is driving her just
For a haircut—THIS is not what we
Think, a second childhood— a child
Has its own world but it is freedom
Itself Phil and Nancy are now losing.

They are losing their minds,
he slowly, she a bit sooner.
But when they sleep at night,
she still pulls the blanket o'er
his thin old body, an act of
love and a proof Nancy is
yet there…

She passed before him—
(my secret prayer filled)
their love still whole,
but oh I miss her wit
everytime I bite into
a slice of cherry pie.

THE PSALM OF ETERNITY

I sing to that I AM,
Beyond time itself,
I sing to the Lord of All,
the Lord of All Worlds
The Lord of Light,
The Father of my soul.

Answer me, O Lord—
This burden of sleep
Lies heavy—I know
I am dreaming, a long
Long dream, but I can
Not rouse my soul…
It sleeps and sleeps
And I can but wait
And wait and wait….

MY FAITH

My faith is different from most,
Whose faith is believing God exists.
I know He is real—I have known
Since I almost died by my own hands,
As I have known that hell is real, and
Far more terrible than any imagined.

I have seen its utter blackness while
My soul—which I had denied like
I had God Himself—was drenched
In torment, that pain beyond pain
Perhaps I had been there before,
For my soul called out, in words
or thought I cannot say—
"How long will it last?"

And then God released my soul
From hell, returned it to my
Near drowned body lying on
The bank of a Vermont river,
Pulled from its rain-gorged
Torrents by a fearless soldier.

So my faith is different, for
Unlike intellectuals wont
To scorn the possibility of
A Being immeasurably
More intelligent than
Their triple-digit I. Q.s,

I can envision a Knowing
That is on a scale
Unfathomable to those
Capable of only one
Thought at a time and
Unable to occupy more
Than a solitary space.

And my faith differs from
Those sure of God's love,
Certain they are among
The Chosen and Heaven's
Gate will swing wide open
For their kind of believer
While shutting tight for
Those of a different ilk:
A Catholic heaven, or

Hindu heaven, or
A Muslim paradise?
Perhaps the Buddha's
Nirvana, or the Tao
Promised Land?
Unlike those faiths,
I cannot exclude,
For I have felt
God's power both
In terror and love,
And so must feel,
Must believe all
Who long for
Heaven's love
Will one day
Arrive....

SONG OF AN OLD MAN

I don't sing of myself—
not anymore,
not since I lost my looks,
half my strength, and
God knows how many brain cells.

There is no joyous song in aging,
there's nothing to look forward to,
unless you like the idea of dying—
and who would? Even the desperate
seek death only as surcease to pain,
not an end in itself, not a destination.

No, there's no upside to growing old,
not like growing up into a world that
itself was malleable, a bit magical—-
scary too, but scary in a good way,
like getting on a roller coaster even
though you have a fear of heights....

No, there's just not a damn thing to
look forward to, or so you think—
and so you tend to look back, to
live again as a youth in memory
and in dreams— ah, dreams!
How you cherish your dreams
now that day-life, so called
'real life' , has become so slow,
so dull, so monotonous ....

But in your dreams you are
sometimes young again, and
sometimes wise and even
brave on occasion— all is
diamond in your dreams,
the dreams of an old man,
the songs of an old man….

SMALLISH THINGS

You hardly notice most of them—
The sweet taste of crisp fall air,
The swing of your arms as your
Legs propel your body freely, you,
An animal that reasons and feels
And remembers and imagines,
All miracles of sentience, all, all
Wonders in a cold uncaring Universe.

And when you talk, the words
Leap from the mind's backroom
Into your wife's mind, or a friend's
Or a stranger asked for directions.
Perhaps you write them down,
A little poem, a gift of soul,
Liked by some, ignored by most—
Still, it spans the unfathomable
Distance between people like
Lightning streaking a darken sky.

Anything created is a wonder.

And you live each day thinking ,
One day I will die, and why, why?
And maybe you think, I'll be gone,
I'll be no more, like I never was….
But you'd be wrong—what to ask
Is: where and in what form do I go?

MIASMA

The world is a paradise,
a melange of desert and forest,
ocean and mountain, of birds
in flight amid cotton clouds
and symphonies of flowers
carpeting God's green earth.

But we are the outsiders,
we are the conflicted species,
never happy for long,
never done....so
we war with ourselves,
then we war with the other.

We deny we wear the same
coat, share the same mind,
feel with the same heart—
we hate—
when loving is easier.
We are so blind, yet
are sure we can see.

Our nature,
our ever so
human nature,
is a miasma
we can never
escape....

IN MY DREAMS

In my dreams I am free
of old-age fears, fears of
falling, fears of losing—
my balance, my money,
my friends, my life…

In my dreams I am
always young again—
who would not want
it so? Who would
not want to go out
to meet the world,
and not have to wait
for the world to come
to you? Girls look at
me like they used to,
in my youth, but still
they look at me and
I feel replete with
life again, and it is
good, even if it is
only in my dreams.

In my dreams I am
REAL—more real
than I feel when I
glance furtively at
the mirror to see
some breathing

remnant staring
back at me— I
almost want to
shout at him,
'Get the hell
outta here!'
But he is already
scared enough,
so I back off and
look forward to
my bedtime when
I will be free of
him, at least for
a little while….

WILL MY SOUL FLY?

Will my soul fly
When I die…
Will my soul soar
O'er the Alps,
The Rockies, the Andes,
And the Himalayas?

Will my soul see
The Aurora Borealis
Finally?

Will my soul
Dive deep, deep
Into the oceans,
Seeing beauty
And creatures
Unknown to
Those who
Live on dry land?

Will my soul slip
Time's iron hold,
Then to skip, at will,
Through the Ages,
Back and forth
Like an unruly child,
(the dream of sages)
Knowing the faces
Of Ceaser stabbed,

Of Joan of Arc burning,
Of Lincoln laughing,
Seeing too the places
Where the lions fed
On the Christian saints,
Where soldiers died
In battles long over,
Where Hitler lied
And Jesus cried?